Becoming *a*
TRUE
SELF

---

40 WAYS IN 40 DAYS

DR. ROSS PORTER

ISBN: 1466208031
ISBN-13: 9781466208032

This book is lovingly dedicated to my parents,
Linda and Ross Porter,
in honor of their 50th wedding anniversary.

Table of Contents

Where have you been?

"One cannot and must not try to erase the past
merely because it does not fit the present."
-Golda Meir

"The past is never completely lost, however extensive
the devastation. Your sorrows are the bricks and mor-
tar of a magnificent temple."
-Gordon Wright

"The past is a guidepost, not a hitching post."
-L. Thomas Holdcroft

"Those who cannot remember the past are condemned
to repeat it."
-George Santayana

Getting to Santa Barbara

"Know thyself."
    -Socrates

Santa Barbara is my favorite city in the whole world. It has nearly perfect weather, beautiful beaches, culture and history, great dining, a spirit of play, and a wonderfully diverse mix of people. I don't live there full-time yet, but that's the goal; the ideal. I get up there as often as possible, and when I leave I miss it all the more.

But how deep would my love for Santa Barbara be if I'd never been anywhere else. If my whole life I'd never seen another city, experienced another city, lived in another city? Sounds great at first, but there's no way I'd have the same level of appreciation and clarity about the Mission, State Street, the Paseo Nuevo, the Museum of Art, Stearns Wharf, the El Encanto, and the countless other treasures my ideal city holds?

Thankfully I have visited and lived in other places, places that were not as good a fit for me, as wonderful, beautiful, or natural. Being able to contrast these places with my ideal place brings greater knowledge and clarity about what works for me, and where I want to end up. And my longing grows. This is a grace.

Your favorite city can serve as a metaphor for your true self. Both are beautiful places you want to get to, and

2

live in, more and more. The true self is you at your very best, the person you are meant to be: most free, alive, relational, authentic, joyful, and creative. Like your ideal city, your true self is what you ultimately want to make your "home."

"Know thyself."

You become a true self by <u>knowing</u> yourself, and then doing something meaningful with the information you gather. Become a student of your own life, studying, exploring, and understanding the good, the bad, and the ugly.

Looking at the "good" is easier and more pleasant, but it's the "bad" and the ugly" that will give you the most useful information. This is where the patterns of self-sabotage lie, where shame and fear still bind you and hold you back.

It takes great courage and humility to do this; to return to, address, and use your pain as a teacher. No one likes to reflect on mistakes and failures, rejection and abandonment, the times people hurt you <u>and the times you hurt yourself</u>. But knowing where you want to go, where you're meant to go, is intimately connected to knowing where you've been.

To truly move forward, you must go back.

Question for reflection: What do you do to know yourself?

3

The potato field

"Integrity is what you do when no one is watching."
   -Tony Dungy

There they stand in the middle of an empty field at dusk. Husband and wife, peasant potato farmers with their tools, wheelbarrow, sacks, and basket surrounding them, their heads are bowed in reverence. The church steeple in the distance along with the title of the painting, *The Angelus,* tells us why. The man and woman have heard the bells calling them to prayer and they've obeyed. They don't have to. God knows they're exhausted from a full day of backbreaking work. Their clothes are dirty, and their expressions sober. Who would blame them for continuing to work in order to more quickly wrap things up for the evening, and maybe cut a few corners? Would it even qualify as cutting corners? For this couple it *would* be, and they'd know it; that settles sit. So they stop.

Jean-Francois Millet's iconic painting is a profound statement about integrity.

Integrity is about what you do when no one's watching. It's about knowing and behaving as you should; not because you must, or because you're afraid, or because you are going to somehow be compensated with acclaim, or a promotion, or a bonus. This moral discipline is the fruit of repetition, of practice...lots of practice.

Aristotle wrote that excellence is a habit, not an act. Being generous on occasion, being merciful when it's convenient, being sacrificial when you know there's a pay-off, being faithful in most ways, loving people who love you...this might pass in today's world as character, but it's still not integrity.

Integrity comes from the word that means "whole" or "complete", and it's about living in ways that make you whole, complete. It's about your walk and your talk being congruent; about consistency, trustworthiness, and truthfulness. Integrity does not ask you to be perfect, but it does demand an ever-deepening, *lived* commitment to good habits; habits that lead to real happiness.

What are the "potato fields" of your life? The places where you are not *immediately* accountable? Where can you "cut corners" morally and probably get away with it: your work, your finances, your interaction with others, the internet, the movies and television shows you watch?

If you're anything like the rest of humankind, you'll have good days and bad days; days you're proud of and days you'd just as soon forget. Work at seeing integrity as a process you begin anew each morning, and evaluate each evening.

And see integrity as a reward in itself; something you strive for *because you can*.

Question for reflection: Who is your model for integrity?

Reading a map

"The map is not the place."
    -S.I. Hayakawa

Have you ever seen an old map of a place you're familiar with? The other day I looked at downtown Los Angeles from the perspective of a map made in 1909. The mapmaker, a gentleman named Worthington Gates, had done a beautiful job charting out the streets, and I'm sure he was quite accurate in his calculations and identifications.

But how helpful would this map be for me today, if I wanted to get from the Cathedral of Our Lady Queen of the Angels to the 5 Freeway, or figure out the fastest route from my lunch meeting on Grand Avenue to a 1:00 appointment on 6th Street? Obviously, not too helpful; Worthington Gates' Los Angeles has grown some. The San Gabriel Mountains still stand in the distance, and the Pacific Ocean shimmers to the west, but roads have been erased, broadened, or renamed. Freeways have been built, sky-scrapers erected, and millions of people have moved in.

Maps need updating from time to time.

Have you ever been in a seemingly innocent conversation about nothing too controversial, and had things take an unexpected turn? Suddenly you find yourself on the giving or the receiving end of a disproportionately emotional blast, and wonder what just happened. You can almost imagine yourself saying, "This territory is vaguely familiar, but I think we made a wrong turn somewhere?" Something like using an outdated map.

The home you were born into, your family-of-origin, was your first experience of community. This still influences you in ways you may not fully recognize. Your family, starting with your mother and father, created a psychological map for you that showed you how to navigate your way through relationships. With this map you learned how to love and like, hope and dream, fear and fight. You watched your family interact, and you experienced the ways they related to you, and the learning went deep...for better and for worse.

You bring this map of relating with you wherever you go. Tone of voice, certain physical characteristics, particular subjects, and personality traits can all be triggers that summon the past and link it powerfully to the present.

At one time, the map your family-of-origin gave you might have worked reasonably well. But the "terrain" of your life has changed.

In times of stress, conflict, and anxiety, however, we can get the past confused with the present. And just like trying to find your way around present day Los Angeles with a map from 1909, you can get very lost.

When pain begins to build, the human instinct is to revert back to what you knew first...your original map for relationships.

However, this map does not have to control you. Just like the mapmaker Worthington Gates would do if he were asked to design a map of downtown Los Angeles today, you can make changes to your map and update the information. The goal is not to avoid the past, an impossible task, but rather to minimize the confusion and pain, and maximize the learning.

Question for reflection: Which maps from your family-of-origin do you need to update?

Favorite Things

"Don't ask yourself what the world needs. Ask yourself what makes you come alive and go do that, because what the world needs is people who have come alive."
  -Howard Thurman

What makes you come alive? Sounds like an unnecessary question for serious-minded people, intent on making the world a better place. Or worse, distracting…after all, life's too short to waste time on "ice-breaker", touchy-feely exercises, right? Let's just focus on responsibility, duty, sacrifice, and leave psycho-babble tripe to encounter groups and high school student-exchange programs.

I've been there, and thought that. So, let me put it differently: When you stand before your Creator someday, will God ask you why you weren't more like Mother Teresa, Mahatma Gandhi, or Abraham Lincoln…or why you weren't more like the person YOU were meant to be? (Hint: It's going to be about you).

"Coming alive" is a challenge that's a good deal more important than one might understand at first; far more than having and maintaining a pulse, and checking the boxes on your daily to-do list. It's fundamentally about becoming the vital, creative person you were meant to be; it's about coming alive.

O.K., so how does this happen? How *does* one come alive?

The most popular response is to change something about your life, shake things up, have a new experience: a memorable vacation, a new hobby, a job change, a new home, a new relationship, bungee jumping. This can help you "come alive" if the new experience can somehow impact you deeply enough to change old patterns. But these experiences are too often like the defibrillator machine and paddles a hospital might use to save someone in cardiac arrest. A quick blast of electricity, and then…

There is another way; one that takes more reflection and time. But it's also more reliable because it taps into something already deep inside you. Rodgers and Hammerstein provide a clue (now there's a sentence I never thought I'd write!).

Recall in *The Sound of Music*, when Julie Andrews sings "My Favorite Things"? She recites a litany of things that help her feel better: raindrops, kittens, kettles, and mittens. But it's a good deal more than a simple list she's racing through; these things have memories and life-giving associations attached to them…as well as instructions.

When I recite a list of just a few of my "favorites" (Jenni, my children, the beach at sunset, lavender, Santa Barbara, Gregorian chant, the Lakers, sycamore trees, pecan pie, Springsteen, Eliot), I come alive, I'm energized, and I'm reminded of what I already know.

Memories are so much more than snapshots of people, places, and things from long ago. They help us learn from the past, process new information, and point the way forward; re-presenting what has worked, what we've cherished, and what we could still embrace. We are reminded of how we've come alive before, and that we don't need to search outside ourselves to really come alive again…for good.

We just need to remember.

Question for reflection: What are your favorite things, and what do they tell you about coming alive?

Socks and shoes

"The devil is in the details."
    -Anonymous

Growing up, I had the amazing experience of going to John Wooden basketball camp for five straight years. For those of you who aren't hoops enthusiasts, let me explain why this was so special.

John Wooden was, is, and always will be considered the greatest college basketball coach of all time. While at U.C.L.A., his teams collected ten NCAA national championships in a 12-year period — seven in a row— an unprecedented achievement. Within this period, his teams won a record 88 consecutive games. He was named national coach of the year six times. The athlete voted the most outstanding college basketball player in America each year is given the John R. Wooden award. The man is an icon.

From ages eight to twelve I got to spend a week each summer with this Hall of Famer, this legend, this master teacher...me and about two hundred other campers.

And what do I remember most clearly about my experiences with the master thirty some odd years later? How to properly put on my socks and shoes.

The first day of camp, the gym was buzzing with excitement. And then John Wooden walked in, the Wizard of Westwood. We all stood and cheered wildly, and he humbly nodded and waved. And then the lessons began. He asked us to take our sneakers and socks off, and spent the next fifteen minutes showing us how to properly put them back on, and why this all mattered.

The first time it happened, I admit I was a little underwhelmed. I figured we'd immediately start playing: running, shooting, and rebounding. Mom had already taught me how to dress myself...I wanted a bit more from Coach. And if I felt that way at eight, how do you think some of the greatest collegiate players of all time felt when he started practice the same way with them?

But John Wooden was a life-coach, not just a basketball coach. He understood that "the devil is in the details." If you don't pay attention to the little things, the seemingly meaningless details as you rush toward action, there will be serious consequences down the road; injuries and failures. I understand now.

Success is built on thoughtful planning, and respect for the fundamentals, and about taking care of first things first. Yes, action must happen, but carefully and with clear purpose. Movement is not the same thing as progress.

I'm still that eight year-old far more often then I care to admit, hurrying to get ahead in the game of life and running the risk of overlooking key details; the clues to what matters most. I act as if I can't afford to slow down; too much to get done. Can you relate?

Maybe it's time to take the socks and shoes off, and start again?

Question for reflection: What are some of the details of your life you need to pay closer attention to?

Knock, knock, knock...

"Let everything happen to you; beauty and terror. Just keep going. No feeling is final."
        -Rainer Maria Rilke

I heard it again today in a counseling session. In fact, if I had a dollar for every time I've heard this sentence in my practice, I'd already be able to afford my beach house.

"I know I shouldn't feel this way."

You shouldn't feel *what* way? Angry, sad, anxious, sexual, bored, skeptical, scared, happy, hopeless? Hmmm....

Few issues are more complicated, less understood, and more routinely mis-used than feelings, emotions. And what I find fascinating is how often they are still seen as threats to stability and general well-being, as intruders to be guarded against.

Feelings move us, stir us, and remind us that our inner worlds hold immense power we are only partially conscious of. Memories and experiences are stored up in the attics of our minds like boxed up books and toys from long ago; dusty and hidden from the light. But then something is said, or done, and in a flash the past is suddenly very present...uninvited. And feelings can leave us vulnerable.

15

So in an effort to protect and control, feelings are repressed, dismissed, or flat-out denied. "I'm fine." "It's no big deal." "It doesn't matter." "This is stupid." "I don't feel anything."

This is psychologically equivalent to hearing the *knock, knock, knock* of the UPS man at the front door with a special delivery for you, and responding by running into the other room, turning up the stereo, and humming loudly until the knocking stops. However, unlike the UPS man, feelings won't go away for long. And your attempts to avoid emotional pain and discomfort will only cause you greater distress.

Feelings are not good or bad. They are value-neutral. What you *do* with feelings can be good or bad, healthy or unhealthy, constructive or destructive. But feelings are simply messengers trying to deliver important information to you about your life. What do you need to explore and heal? What do you need to change? What do you need to continue doing?

No feeling is final. But the damage done by not heeding messages from your interior world can be.

Question for reflection: What feelings are you most uncomfortable with?

Careful where you dig

"You cannot love what you do not know."
            –St. Thomas Aquinas

This past summer King Tutankhamen visited our city again. It had been over twenty years since the boy king, who died in 1339 B.C., was on tour along with artifacts from his tomb. As impressive as the exhibit was, though, I found the story of his discovery as interesting as the treasures that lay inside his almost perfectly in-tact final resting place. Howard Carter, the English archaeologist who found Tut's tomb, had searched carefully, persistently, purposefully for ten years in the blazing Egyptian desert. And when he finally found the entrance to the tomb, almost accidentally, the work was still not finished.

Locating a treasure is not worth very much if you destroy it in the unearthing process. So, Carter and his team ever so gently, almost reverently, explored the interior of the tomb, and the person who lay within, foot by foot, observing, studying, learning with great respect. After ten years of searching, you can imagine how much Carter might have been tempted to rush, to hurry, to take control of his find and exploit it for personal gain. But he maintained a remarkably unhurried and cautious pace, not wanting to damage in any way such a precious find. The process was more important to him than any individual agenda. Howard Carter's approach to King Tut and his world serves as an apt analogy for how to love your loved ones. In relationships, we must be careful when digging...archaeology with a heart!

Wanting to explore the mystery of those you love is an essential part of intimacy and friendship. If you're not curious about the lives of your core people there's a problem.

"You cannot love what you do not know."

In order to make discoveries, you must do some digging into the past; not everything lies on the surface. In exploring your loved one's life, you will sooner or later come upon pockets of pain, where shame about past experiences and guilt about past choices lie. And when this pain is accessed, when your loved one is suddenly feeling vulnerable and frightened, it is imperative to proceed with caution.

We are not wounded in isolation and we do not heal in isolation, so this unearthing is a crucial part of becoming a true self. Secrets bind but truth sets us free, as we feel accepted and loved as we are, and realize that we are bigger than our pain.

Just remember that discovering a treasure is wasted if, in the handling, it is destroyed.

Question for reflection: How are you at "archaeology with a heart"?

Facing pain

"There is no coming to consciousness without pain."
    -Carl Jung

Jung is right, of course. There is no coming to consciousness, no "waking up to reality" if you will without pain. Whether it arrives physically, emotionally, or spiritually, pain will come knocking. C.S. Lewis once said, "God whispers to us in our pleasure and shouts to us in our pain." This is reality, this is life on planet earth. Lots of wonderful, beautiful, fun, loving experiences, but always with a pinch of pain tossed into the mix here and there (and sometimes even more than just here and there). This is not Heaven.

The point of this life is to learn how to love and grow up, to help others learn to love and grow up, and to prepare for eternity. This doesn't happen without pain. Sure wish it did, but it doesn't.

But as someone who feels pain, as someone who works with people in pain all the time, and as someone who (like millions of others around the world) is trying to embrace all that is Holy Week, *simply feeling pain is not enough*.

People in pain can be quite dangerous, destructive, crazed...like wounded animals. They have not come to "consciousness," to awareness and mindfulness. Or maybe they have, and concluded that objective reality is not what they're willing or able to embrace.

19

What do we do with pain when it comes? This is the key question. Do we pretend like we don't feel it? Do we get busy, compulsive, frantic with activity? Do we isolate? Do we go to war against real or perceived enemies (anger is a popular hiding place for those attempting to manage pain)?

Or do we feel, and bring the pain into relationship with trusted others (asking for accountability, guidance, support, and love). Feel, and work to place the pain in a larger context of meaning and purpose (what can be learned about the world, human nature, and all that I have to be grateful for?). Feel, and choose to let the pain educate us about where we need to grow up (immaturity, entitlements, and illusions). Feel, and choose to purify, mortify the parts of us that need to die (pride, sloth, greed...shoot, just choose your own favorite deadly sin and insert here)?

Life is difficult. Pain is inevitable. No use denying. So let's learn what we can, seize the opportunity for transformation, face reality as head-on as possible, stay connected to life-giving people and institutions, and recognize that the pain we feel (however debilitating, terrifying, crushing, or maddening) is only part of the much larger reality of our lives. Let's not hide... for our sakes, for the sakes of our loved ones, and for the sake of this hurting world. Because if we can summon enough courage to live in truth, pain will not have the final word. And resurrection will become much more than a theory.

Question for reflection: What do you typically do with your pain?

20

In the beginning....

"If you would understand anything, observe its beginning and its development."
      -Aristotle

I didn't think the assignment was going to be very difficult. "Tell me about your family history. Where were your ancestors from, where did they settle when they first arrived in America, and what did they do for a living." Basic information, straightforward, easily shared, right? Wrong.

A disturbing number of students couldn't even tell me much about their grandparents' pasts, let alone foremothers and forefathers from three or four generations back. "We don't really talk about the past." "How would I know?" "What does that have to do with me?"

It got me wondering how many of today's teenagers are a-historical: unaware and/or unconcerned about their roots, their family histories. And what the cost is.

"If you would understand anything, observe its beginning and its development."

We cannot know ourselves, understand ourselves, simply by looking at ourselves. This is simplistic at best, and runs the real risk of feeding a culture that is already startlingly shallow and narcissistic.

21

Knowing the stories of those who came before us… appreciating the sacrifice, the courage, and the perseverance of our ancestors…is a crucial part of knowing our own stories. A generation that is not meaningfully rooted in its history, and grateful for a foundation to build on, cannot grow to full maturity.

Question for reflection: How much of your family story do you know?

A dangerous fish

"Action expresses priorities."
    -Mohandas Gandhi

I feel the need to offer a disclaimer at the outset of this reflection: *I am not against thinking deeply or feeling deeply*. I'd hope that my career choices, and the twenty-three years I spent in school would support this position. And I might add that as a melancholic temperament, I naturally appreciate interiority and reflection. But there can be too much of a good thing.

Do you know the expression "following a red herring"? It comes from a medieval technique used by dog owners to train young scent hounds. A fish, typically a herring, would be soaked in brine or well-smoked and then dragged along a trail by the trainer until the puppy learned to follow the scent. But the goal was not to have the dog follow the strongest scent, but rather the original scent…the one identified as crucial to the search. So the trainer would introduce other scents, and eventually use the red herring to try and confuse the dog. Thus, a "red herring" has come to be known as something that diverts one away from tracking and locating the identified target.

Thinking deeply and feeling deeply by themselves do not lead to change. In fact, they can lead away from it. Self-obsession, isolation, stuckness? Quite possibly. But not change. I believe this is a major reason why counseling fails, even when clients show up, and keep showing up; all the talking and all the feeling doesn't get translated into a meaningful plan of action that is *moved* on.

People change for the good, *and for good*, by living differently; by reflecting on their thoughts and feelings *and then putting them into action*.

And action expresses priorities.

Assume that a stranger was observing your life, day in and day out, for several months *without you actually knowing it*. At the conclusion of the study, would he have an accurate picture of what you <u>say</u> you value most, based solely on your actions?

"I love her." What are you going to do about it? *"I hate my job."* What are you going to do about it? *"I regret my relationship with my mom."* What are you going to do about it? *"I need to break that habit."* What are you going to do about it?

Don't let thinking deeply and feeling deeply become red herrings. Use them to better track the real target, *which is right action*.

Question for reflection: Where do you need to take action?

Anger Management

"It is wise to direct your anger towards problems -- not people; to focus your energies on answers -- not excuses."
     -William Arthur Ward

Can you name one person in your life who is a healthy model for anger? I'm sure you can picture plenty of people...probably too many people... who rage or repress, get passive-aggressive or isolate with their anger. And after the fact make excuses for their bad behavior.

But do you have a healthy model for how to do anger well?

Anger is an emotion denied by many and feared by most because of its potential to harm. "Anger hurts people." "I don't trust myself when I'm angry." "Anger is a sin."

Yes, anger can be used to hurt people. Yes, if I don't know how to work with my anger I probably should be unsure of myself with it. And yes, anger can lead to evil.

But anger can also lead to healing, self-control, and goodness. And most of all it can lead to intimacy. And it's the issue of intimacy I want to focus on here.

Much time in counseling and spiritual direction is spent helping one process through anger; identify the grievance, feel the wound, and develop a plan to confront the other. And this can all be fruitful. But if the process never goes beyond this, a critical step is missing.

In your anger with another, how are you angry with yourself? In your anger with another, how have you hurt yourself? In your anger with another, how have you compromised your goodness, your truth, and your dignity? Ask care-fully and thoughtfully.

Use your anger to explore how you need to be more gentle, more peaceful, more joyful, and more mindful of all that truly matters.

When you return to your "side of the street", focus on yourself and your own unfinished business, the deeper process of responsibility-taking can really begin. Then the unpleasant experience of anger (giving and/or receiving) becomes an opportunity to learn and grow, and your more authentic understanding of self will certainly be a blessing for those around you.

In the end, the battle is not about the other, it's about you.

Question for reflection: What does anger look like in your life?

Living with a big cat

"We don't see things as they are, we see them as we are."
        -Anais Nin

Are you familiar with the saying, "The tiger you know is better than the tiger you don't know?" It originated in India, with townspeople that lived on the edge of jungles inhabited by tigers. Inevitably, a tiger would wander out of the jungle and through the town, looking for food. This was certainly an immediate danger, but over time the town got to know the tiger's habits, his routines, and when he would come calling. They chose not to kill the tiger, because they knew that another would soon replace it, and bring new habits they were unfamiliar with. This new tiger would be more dangerous than the old because the new one would be unpredictable.

This "settling mentality" may be the right strategy for Indian towns dealing with tiger problems, but it is a slow death for human beings.

"No, I'm not terribly happy, or satisfied, but it could be worse."

We all get into ruts, and stay in ruts for many reasons, *but at the core is a fear of change*. We are always free to make changes, big and small, and this incredible gift can be terrifying. No excuses: we are responsible for our lives. We have choices. We don't have to settle.

27

But we must risk, in order to grow. And risk brings us face to face with the tiger we don't know. We might fail, we might get hurt, we might be rejected.

One of my favorite scenes in the Bible is Jesus confronting this fear of change, this help-rejecting attitude, when He sized up the paralytic at the Pool of Bethsaida: "Do you want to be healed?" Jesus is clearly addressing more than the physical hardship of the man, or else He could rightly be criticized for cruelty. After all, the man was not at fault for being paralyzed. The man had been in this paralyzed state for many years, a state of physical paralysis, but even more binding a state of emotional paralysis. He needed to get his head in the right place. He needed an attitude adjustment. He had grown too comfortable in his pain and discomfort, too comfortable in his role as the helpless victim of life circumstances. He had quit.

How much of this settling mentality has crept into your life, along with the help-rejecting, freedom-denying spirit that always accompanies it? What have you accepted as permanent and unchangeable: unhappiness, compulsive habits, rude behavior, avoidant ways of living (or more accurately, *hiding*)?

Tigers can be frightening, but not as frightening as a life of regret.

Question for reflection: Where in your life have you "settled"?

Where Are You Now?

"The present contains all that there is. It is holy ground;
for it is the past, and it is the future."
-Alfred North Whitehead

"One of the most tragic things I know about human nature is that all of us tend to put off living. We are all dreaming of some magical rose garden over the horizon instead of enjoying the roses that are bloom-ing outside our windows today."
-Dale Carnegie

"No longer forward nor behind
I look in hope or fear;
But grateful, take the good I find,
The best of now and here."
-John Greenleaf Whittier

"Escapees into the past and the future have one thing in common:

they do not take the present seriously.
The past cannot be regained,
although we can learn from it; the future
is not yet ours even though we
must plan for it…Time is now.
We have only today."
-Charles Hummel

A thing of beauty

"Earth is crammed with heaven, and every common bush afire with God..."
     -E.B. Browning

It was definitely not my finest hour. I can make excuses; we were both in graduate school, we were both working multiple jobs, we were both stressed, money was tight. But I was still a knucklehead. Jenni and I had been back from our honeymoon all of one week, and I came home one evening to find my sweet wife joyfully arranging flowers in a crystal vase. My parents had sent us twenty dollars in a "welcome home" card, and she'd gone out and bought a bright, beautiful bouquet with it.

I immediately questioned my new bride's judgment, stating quite rationally that the $20 could have paid for five or six dinners (at that time we were on an "all-pasta/all-the-time" meal plan). It could have paid for a month of electricity. It could have paid for a month of cable. "And besides," I concluded, "the flowers will be dead in three days." (Blank Stare).

After Jenni paused for a moment, she calmly explained that life wasn't just about paying bills.

Wife: 1, Husband: O

Beauty matters. It matters because it awakens the senses, celebrates life, and elevates the spirit. And if it did nothing but this, it would matter a lot. Can you even imagine a day without beautiful colors, or music, or shapes, or smells? But beauty does something more, and the clue is in its passing nature.

Beauty is always passing away. By nature, it's transitory. Flowers wilt, sunsets set, blue skies get smoggy or gray, rainbows vanish, scents dissipate, smiles disappear, and even physical beauty diminishes with time. And this is good, because if beauty never faded, we'd worship it. We'd stay fixated on the material, and not see the eternal purpose it ultimately serves. Beauty points to the One Who Created it, the One Who is eternal, the One Who is calling us to a beauty that doesn't end.

Love beauty, and through it love the One Who thinks you are beautiful.

Question for reflection: What is beautiful to you?

Accounting 101

"Accountability breeds response-ability."
        -Stephen R. Covey

Talk about your wake-up call!   Dr. Alfred Nobel, whose name has become synonymous with peace, was confronted one morning with his own obituary after a newspaper confused him with his recently deceased brother. *"The merchant of death is dead,"* the headline shouted. *"Dr. Alfred Nobel, who became rich by finding ways to kill more people faster than ever, died yesterday."*

Nobel, the inventor of dynamite, was deeply disturbed that he would be remembered this way. And because of this experience he ended up designating the bulk of his massive estate to the establishment of the Nobel Prizes.

Accountability comes in many forms, even obituaries. And we will all have the chance to answer its call, sooner or later....answer for our actions, or inactions. "Accountability breeds response-ability," because the challenge to live in truth comes from outside of us, reveals to us our psychological and spiritual blind spots, and stretches us beyond where we'd go if left to our own devices.

But what do you get when you answer to no one? And even worse, that in your isolation and denial your discernment is lacking? What you get is an increasingly large segment of American culture.

A significant amount of research suggests that Americans don't understand the true nature of accountability, and are increasingly likely to fall prey to the phenomenon known as the "self-serving bias." What does that mean? People will show a reliable tendency to interpret events in ways that are most favorable to them, or show them in the best possible light, *even when objective facts don't justify these judgments*.

If I get the job it's because I'm wonderful, if I don't it's because I was discriminated against. If I stay with my wife, it's because I'm wonderful, if I leave it's because she wasn't meeting my needs. If my son excels in school it's because he's my son, and I'm wonderful, if he rebels it's because of the school.

This is consistent with what Paul Vitz has called "self-ism", and what Christopher Lasch has called "the culture of narcissism."

I can decide that I want to drive to San Francisco. I can have a high-performance car, a confident attitude, and even know what I want to do when I get there. But if I go south instead of north, and then east instead of west, I'm not going to end up in San Francisco. And all of my positive self-talk and ego-strength won't change the fact that I'm headed in the wrong direction. In fact, the longer I go without a clue, the more lost I'll get.

We routinely seek out and follow trustworthy information about diets, movies, clothes, restaurants, fitness regimens, electronic devices, and finances. Should we not do at least as much for the direction of our lives, and our eternal souls?

Question for reflection: Who do you answer to?

Sharing the rough draft

"Communication works for those who work at it."
-John Powell

For ten years, my wife Jenni taught English composition to high school students. Many would compare this act of bravery to lion taming or crocodile wrestling. It's not that high school students are terrible, in fact they can be charming and inspiring. It's that more and more kids don't read anymore. Text messages and emails don't count. And to write well, one must read well.

Reading gives one a sense of the flow of words, the development of ideas, and the complex relationship of characters in any given story. To help her students write better, Jenni would break them into groups of two or three and have them read *out loud* to each other the rough drafts of their essays. This was done early in the process, before they had spent too much time traveling down a wrong road. She'd often ask them, "How does it *sound* so far?" Are my thoughts and ideas making sense, and am I headed for a well-developed and coherent conclusion, or have I gotten off track?

We are constantly having internal monologues about relationships. "I think my wife is mad at me because I didn't ask her about her day?" "My friend must be bored with me because I see him yawn all the time." "I wonder if I'm doing a good job with this assignment?"

Our thoughts and our feelings give us an initial "read" on a given situation, something like a rough draft, but these assumptions are often untested. Is this absolute fact, or is it just something I think or feel to be true?

Communication, and intimacy, must be a dialogue not a monologue.

Too often a "rough draft" bounces around in our heads and hearts, but doesn't get voiced until we're pretty far down the road toward a conclusion. Maybe we don't share because we're too busy, maybe it's because we're afraid of what's really going on, and maybe we keep our internal monologues to ourselves because we're insecure about possibly needing anything. Whatever the reason, it's dangerous. We're practicing emotionally isolating behavior that slowly weakens intimacy. Fears creep in, and we become increasingly likely to behave *as if* our assumptions are actual realities.

And over time these false assumptions have been left to harden like concrete. Thus, it takes much work to chisel away the layers of defensiveness and get to the truth. So much pain and loneliness could have been avoided if the rough drafts had been "read" out loud, brought into the light.

Your thoughts and feelings are very important. They give you meaningful information about who you are and where you've been, but they are not always an accurate read on life going on around you. *Your thoughts and feelings are not infallible.*

Share what's in your head, share what's in your heart... early and often. "Let me read my rough draft to you." "How does it sound so far?" "Have I got it right, or is my conclusion faulty?"

And don't just stop at reading the rough draft of your thoughts and feelings out loud; edit, revise, re-write! The final draft is yours, but it should include plenty of feedback...especially from those you love best.

Question for reflection: Who do you share your "rough drafts" with?

In my opinion, it's often far better to bite your tongue & keep your monologue (thoughts) to yourself until you've really gotten past it. A word once spoken cannot ever be retrieved or erased!

It's not JUST about you!

"We live our lives like chips in a kaleidoscope, always parts of patterns that are larger than ourselves and somehow more than the sum of their parts."
    -Salvador Minuchin

Here's a commencement address I'd love to hear spoken gently, lovingly, and with real conviction to all graduates, at all graduations around the world: at high schools, colleges, and graduate schools:

It's about you, but it's not just about you." I believe this message would be good for those in the audience to hear as well.

You matter. You are special. You are unique. And so are the other 6.92 billion human beings you need to learn how to share this planet with.

One needs to be careful at times of great celebration not to get preachy. Actually there's no great time to get preachy. But a commencement ceremony is a particularly strategic place to point out the wonderfully complex, inter-relatedness of life, and then to challenge any folks who might still be listening to try to think at least as much about others as they do about themselves.

We are, as Minuchin points out, like chips in a kaleidoscope...part of a pattern much bigger than we can even imagine. We don't get smaller with this realization, but our understanding of the world can get a whole lot bigger. And this is a good start.

In truth, there is no such thing as an "independent" person, a self-made person, a lone-ranger. You did not create yourself, you did not create the talents you've been blessed with, and you did not create the natural world you live in. Yes, you have the opportunity and responsibility to develop the life and talents you were given, and embrace the world around you, but this doesn't happen in isolation either. You stand on the shoulders of others, who have sacrificed, struggled, and persevered in making your world better.

This is a ridiculously obvious insight, but insight has never guaranteed change. And in a culture that is increasingly privatized, and thus increasingly splintered and alienated, it's best not to assume about anything that's important.

So what do we do with this insight? We recognize the gift, we recognize the giver, and then we start saying thank you; thoughtfully, sincerely, and continuously. Life is a gift, health is a gift, love and friendship are gifts, freedom is a gift, truth is a gift, beauty is a gift, work is a gift, play is a gift, triumphs are a gift, struggles are a gift. And the opportunity to make a difference for the Good with all you've been given is perhaps the greatest gift of all.

Gratitude opens us up to all that is good, and to a deeper knowing that our world is not accidental, but Providential. It's about you, but it's not just about you. And you should be grateful!

Question for reflection: Who deserves a thank-you from you today?

Working it out

"It's not the job you do, it's how you do the job."
-Anonymous

I awoke at 6 A.M. this morning with my newly attached crown suddenly detached, and rattling around in my mouth like a little piece of hard candy. Normally I'd have the self-restraint to wait until a decent hour to call about this, but nerve pain has a way of blowtorching certain social niceties.

I vaguely recalled my dentist encouraging me to contact his colleague who would be standing in for him over this holiday weekend if any problems arose.

So, I called Dr. Howard Gottlieb's emergency number, expecting to get his answering service. The man himself picked up. Now remember, its Saturday morning, he's not my dentist, and did I mention that it was 6 A.M. on a holiday weekend? "No problem, I'm on the job. Now let's get you in and fixed up."

I wasn't on pain medication, so I know for sure that he actually said these words.

Honestly, if I listed all the virtues, the good habits, that make the world a better place, professionalism would not be in my top twenty...maybe not even in my top fifty. But it should be. Consider the powerfully positive impact doing your job with a spirit of excellence 40-50 hours a week, fifty some odd weeks a year, can have on the world around you.

Professionalism is not the job you do, it's how you do the job.

It includes competency, *but it's much more than just competency*. One who practices professionalism sees human beings and not just tasks, seizes opportunities to care and not just profit, and attends *at least as much* to what can't be tallied on a spread sheet as what can.

That's why professionalism is a virtue; it makes you a better person, not just a successful person.

So, in due time I arrived at the office and the good doctor was waiting for me. He was pleasant, prompt, and proficient, and in 45 minutes had me on my way. "How much do I owe you" I asked? "Nothing," he answered. "Dr. Ford would do the same for me if I was on vacation."

As I left I thanked him once more, and told him how very grateful I was for his professionalism. He smiled and shook his head. "Hey, this is what I do."

Well, that's true...and then some!

Question for reflection: How hard do you work at professionalism?

Too Much Reality

"Humankind cannot stand too much reality."
   -T.S. Eliot

I have not been asked to give a speech at Rutgers University. I suspect I never will be either. Not too surprising.

What might be considered surprising, however, is the person who recently was asked.

There is so much that disturbs me about Rutgers University's decision to pay Nicole "Snooki" Polizzi of "Jersey Shore" reality television fame $32,000 to speak to the student body about her "GTL lifestyle" (that would be Gym-Tanning-Laundry for the uninitiated). I begin with the judgement that she was someone worth bringing on campus at all (the major takeaway from her talk: "Study hard, but party harder"); and that she was paid with money from a mandatory student activity fee; and that her appearance fee was more than the fee paid to Nobel Prize winning author Toni Morrison for giving the commencement address at the very same school one month later. I could go on.

My first instinct was to go on the offensive; attack the messenger. "Snooki" is so easy for sensible people to dislike, to blame, to vilify for her part in this cultural drift toward banality and worse. But after a good old fashioned, self-righteous rant, I realized that I was

44

doing some classic scapegoating. This character is a creation, not a creator. She is a symptom of the illness, not the illness. Even before her fifteen minutes of fame end, there will be (and already is) another loud, crude, exhibitionistic "Snooki", or Brody, or Sheen, or take-your-pick Kardashian, or Paris ready to squat in the role of "reality star" for the next fifteen minutes.

My second instinct was defensive; dismiss the message because of the messenger. "Snooki" is a bad joke, and the Rutgers decision to invite her is just an aberration. I'd never ask Snooki to speak, pay her to speak, or listen to her speak. This isn't my reality. And the vast majority of the world is with me on this one, no doubt. "Distracted from distraction by distraction...filled with fancies and empty of meaning." All the noise, and toys, and hysteria, and fighting, and booze, and vomit, and sex, and plastic surgery...

But if this is true, then why am I so worked up? Why, if this person and this decision are so pathetic and irregular, am I so angry about it? This isn't about me, right? Not my reality? Not connecting with my story at all?

Here's a crazy thought. What if reality television was not primarily inexpensive programming material intended to numb America into a moral stupor, but rather a sophisticated series of commentaries hidden in the guise of trash, meant to graphically expose humankind's frailty...both poignant and horrible at the same time?

45

Maybe I shouldn't pretend to be so surprised about Snooki, and Rutgers?

The recently beatified Mother Teresa of Calcutta was once asked why she did what she did. Her answer: "Because I have a Hitler inside me." She is a saint. I can't get there yet (mostly because I don't consistently want to get there yet). But what I can admit to today is that I have a "Snooki" inside me.

Like "Snooki", and the folks at Rutgers and elsewhere who find her fascinating, I have a fallen nature; a fundamental fault line which reminds me in little and big ways as life rocks and rolls that often my reality does not conform with Reality. Like "reality television", my life is still too filled with staged encounters, and drama, and sensationalism, and youtube-worthy moments of puff and emptiness.

Too much Reality for my reality.

To use Eliot's words once more, I too seek to be "distracted from distraction by distraction", in order to not rest too long at the "still point of the turning world." And all the while the God Who Uses Everything whispers that I am very much like those people...the Jersey Shore, Real Housewives, Kardashian, The Hills, Celebrity Rehab people. I would still too often prefer to talk about myself, to observe others (taking particular interest in their mistakes), to bask in the illusion of control, to pretend to have all the answers, and to subtly feel superior in an acceptably "Christian" way.

And maybe you can relate? Just a little? So now what?

I'd like to turn to the solution, to quickly switch the focus to what we can all do to put the reality television dimension of our own lives in the rear view mirror. I'd really like to do this. Because humankind cannot stand too much reality.

Question for reflection: When are you most unreal?

Just the facts?

"And now you know the <u>rest</u> of the story!"
 -Paul Harvey

It's Springtime, so allow me to recall my greatest personal baseball achievement. I got an RBI single off a major league pitcher, in an all-star game, before a packed, standing-room only stadium. I'm serious. It was a letter-high fast ball. The pitcher was Bret Saberhagen, two-time Cy Young award winner and MVP of the 1985 World Series. He was to end up with 167 wins in his career, and pitch in three Major League all-star games.

Everything about this story is true. And it's not enough. Because facts need to be placed in the larger context of life, of the larger story, in order for understanding to happen...

Bret and I were 12 years-old. The all-star game was Tarzana vs. Reseda. The packed stadium was the Encino-Tarzana Little League field. Oh, and he also struck me out two times that day. Bret would go on to achieve baseball greatness, and I would not.

People can present facts and still not tell the whole story. Facts can clarify, but they can also confuse. And if understanding isn't sought and found, relationships will suffer and even end.

"All I said was 'The Jones' are going to Hawaii this summer'." But what was your intent?

"I have to work these long hours in order to support this family." But what about your other commitments?

"I've told my son a hundred times not to do that." But have you heard what he's been trying to tell you?

In times of conflict, the list of facts presented are all too often strategically chosen, carefully airbrushed, and part of a self-centered agenda; like an attorney trying to win a case in court. Understanding is lost in the battle to be "right." And "right" can leave one feeling very alone.

What do you want out of relationships? Do you want to find love and happiness? Do you want to grow, and help others grow as well? Do you want to find real peace? Then you'd do well to seek more than just facts. Seek to understand and to be understood.

"What's your take on this?" "Tell me what your thoughts are." "Help me understand where you're coming from." "What am I not hearing?"

What's the story…the whole story?

Question for reflection: Do you try to understand the whole story?

The "If" word

"A stiff apology is a second insult.... The injured party does not want to be compensated because he has been wronged; he wants to be healed because he has been hurt."
    -G.K. Chesterton

Last week I read of another public figure who began his feeble attempt at an apology for bad behavior with the phrase, "If I offended anyone…" This is what Chesterton would call a "stiff apology." I would call it insincere.

I'd like to simply explain this as another narcissistic famous person being too full of himself to actually practice humility. He was apologizing because his manager or publicist told him to. I think my analysis is probably true, but there's more to it than this…it goes deeper. Because the struggle to offer a real apology is not a famous person issue, it is a human being issue; mothers and fathers, sons and daughters, husbands and wives, friends and foes.

"If I offended anyone…", "If my words hurt you…", "If you took it that way…"

When it comes to apologizing, the "if" word is a really bad word.

A sincere apology is a rare thing indeed; no "ifs", no "ands", and no "buts". Why? I think the answer involves several issues, including immaturity, fear, pride, and indifference. But I'm most interested in what it says about how one sees relationships.

Transactional. Conditional. Quid pro quo. "This for that"; I'll give you an apology because the consequence might cost me something. You might get angry with me, you might try and hurt me back, you might hassle me with more of your boring feelings.

So, I'll offer something that sounds polite and hopefully that will cover the "damages." Yes, it is very general, and it needs to be. *Specifics* challenge me to reflect on what I've done, and what I need to take responsibility for. And I'm as *dis*interested in exploring my motives as I am in empathizing with your feelings.

"Why" takes time. "Why" takes energy. "Why" asks me to be vulnerable.

A lousy apology, one that comes from the head and not the heart and is grounded in pride and not humility, does nothing to help heal the wound my words or deeds have caused. In fact, it makes matters worse. My lack of genuine care and interest in the relationship is made even more obvious. In the end (and probably in the beginning and middle, too) it is still about me and my feelings, not you and yours.

Everyone makes mistakes. This is human, and understandable. But I can't be forgiven if I don't really think I need to be, and don't really ask to be. And I can't be trusted either.

Question for reflection: Do you apologize well?

If you're going through hell...

"If you're going through hell, keep going."
        -Winston Churchill

Recently, I found myself lost while driving in a part of town I was not familiar with. I'd like to blame Mapquest for faulty information, but the truth is that I left the directions at home. I'm usually pretty good at navigating, and had a general sense of where I needed to go, so I decided to journey forth anyway. But as I neared my destination, I took the wrong off-ramp, and then several wrong turns. After several minutes of wandering into one dead-end after another, I had to admit that I was officially lost.

The bigger issue, however, was that I'd also somehow managed to find my way into the most unsafe neighborhood I'd ever been in, complete with broken street lights, drug deals, and gangbangers congregating on street corners. I was confused about my surroundings, but clear that to stop moving, to park and sit, to curse my lot and quit trying to find my way out would be unhealthy in more ways than one. I was not in hell, but it was close enough.

"If you're going through hell, keep going."

I gathered myself and began again to look for street signs and landmarks that would point me in the right direction and re-orient me. Carefully, I exited this dark labyrinth and eventually entered a safer neighborhood where I could pull over and ask for help.

Life will sometimes feel like one dead-end after another, in a dangerous neighborhood, without a way out. Regardless of who you are, you will on occasion find yourself in hell. You can set out with a fair amount of confidence that where you're intending to go is where you're going to end up. You may even have your directions right there with you. But unexpected twists and turns will leave you confused and unsettled; lost. And the pain that accompanies the experience of being "lost" can feel like hell; overwhelming, terrifying, hopeless.

Perhaps it is an addiction, or a heartbreaking marriage, or an out-of-control child. Maybe you've lost your job, or your health? "Will the disappointment ever end?" "Will I ever get a break?" "Will these hard times pass?" Yes…but only if you keep going.

See the "signs", the "landmarks", and the "maps" of your life. What has worked for you in the past and what hasn't? What gives you peace and what doesn't? What affirms life, and what doesn't. And KEEP GOING: toward people who are trustworthy, wise, and generous; toward sources of wisdom that communicate eternal truth to you; toward a future that allows you to live your giftedness with joy.

And hell will soon enough be in your rear view mirror.

Question for reflection: What are the hells you've found yourself in, and what have you done?

Think small

"A new command I give you: Love one another."
        -Jesus the Christ

Mother Teresa, the saint of Calcutta, was fond of saying, "We can do no great things, only small things with great love." Mother, no doubt, had a bit of the trickster in her...for she knew better than most that when you do something with great love, it ceases to be small. Love is eternal, and it infuses everything it touches with Eternity. Can't get much bigger than that.

Her challenge, historically known as the "little way," is a great one for all of us as we face the New Year. I believe that people too often think that anything less than finding a cure for cancer, or solving the economic crisis, or donating a ton of money to some well-deserving non-profit organization is not significant enough to tilt the world. But the reality is that when you love another, you move yourself and that person toward Heaven.

BIG tilt.

Start with yourself and those closest to you, and work your way outward from the center. What little things can you do today, right now: offer a smile? An affirming word? A quick prayer? A menial task done without being asked? A "love letter" on a post-it? Some minor sacrifice for another that stretches you a bit?

Resist the temptation to think that "little acts of love" don't matter, and strive for consistency. Resist the temptation to get perfectionistic about your actions, and move in freedom. Resist the temptation to need someone/anyone/everyone to notice how loving you're being. This plan is good for you, naturally and supernaturally. And the fact that God notices and is pleased is a pretty good reason to be at peace also!

Every day, make a decision to do little things with great love...or as much love as you can muster up. And the world will become a better place, big time!

Question for reflection: What little thing can you do today with great love?

Heart-strong

"Courage is not simply one of the virtues, but the form of every virtue at the testing point."
     -C.S. Lewis

When one speaks of courage, images that jump to mind are of heroic action: the first responders on 9/11, a teen-aged St. Joan of Arc leading the army of France into battle, the soldiers who stormed the beaches at Normandy. Certainly these are all outstanding examples, but can also lead people to believe that courage only happens on the largest of stages, with lives in the balance. We miss the full beauty of this virtue if we don't recognize that courage is just as fully presented in the "little things"...victories that can't be quantified. *Victories that can only be measured by the heart.*

In fact, the word Courage comes from the Latin for "Heart". Courage takes the "thought" to do good, and puts it into action. To resist giving in to obstacles, and to take positive action...that's courage.

And there was plenty of courage, heart, on display recently at a high-school baseball diamond.

My dear friend and colleague Joe Sikorra was there with his son John. John is blind, and struggling with the devastating effects of Batten disease, a neurodegenerative disorder. But his dream has always been to play high school baseball. He's been on the team as a "coach" this year, but that wasn't enough. He wanted to hit, and he wanted to run, and he wanted to score.

So, yesterday at the start of the game, the manager chose John to be the leadoff hitter. The visiting team took the field, honoring the moment with their cooperation. A ball tee was placed at home plate, and Joe led John to it...and then stood back and let him swing for the fences. Blast-off! As John, led by his father, rounded the bases the crowd rose and cheered, a boy's dream was realized, and this weary world seemed just a bit brighter.

Coming to grips with a catastrophic medical condition would drive most into hiding, swamped by fear, anger, anxiety, grief...and retreating into a less public forum to await the inevitable. And no one would have blamed the Sikorras for doing just that. But they chose instead to feel the feelings and move forward, to embrace the life they'd been given, and make the most of as many moments as they could.

Courage. It's the virtue of battlefields and burning buildings. But yesterday it was also the virtue of a high school baseball diamond, when a beautiful young man running short on time and his proud father grabbed hands and together charged past fear, and into an immortal moment that all of Heaven cheered...along with a couple of hundred people on earth.

Question for reflection: Where do you need to practice courage in your life?

Who are you listening to?

"It's not that I'm so smart, it's just that I stay with problems longer."
     -Albert Einstein

Lucille Ball was dismissed from a drama class, with the penetrating insight: "She's wasting her time here. She's too shy to put her best foot forward."

A brand new band calling themselves The Beatles was rejected by the first recording company they approached. The reasons given? "We don't like their sound. And besides, guitar music is on the way out."

Abraham Lincoln had two failed businesses, suffered a nervous breakdown, experienced the death of his fiancé, and lost eight elections.

Michael Jordan was cut from his Freshman high school basketball team.

Thomas Edison was told by a teacher that he was "too stupid to learn anything."

Walt Disney was fired from a newspaper job because, as the termination report read, "He lacks imagination and has no original ideas."

The longer I live, the more I realize that people who succeed in life are people who are courageous enough to risk failure and loss, and are able to pick themselves up and get back in the race when they inevitably do get knocked down; they persevere.

And a critical part of risking failure and persevering in our efforts, of persisting in the face of obstacles and creating something beautiful with the gifts we've been given is who we choose to listen to. Which voices do we filter out, and which voices do we let in?

How do we do this discerning? Start with a simple rule of thumb: spend more and more time with life-giving people, and less and less time with life-taking people. Too simple? I'm amazed at how many people don't follow this advice. There is confusion about responsibility ("I must spend time with this person, respect this person, take care of this person"), or history ("It's not always bad"), or even what it means to be a good person ("I shouldn't be angry, sad, tired, happy"). Crazy? No, just fear-based. The people you surround yourself with, and let in, can absolutely make you or break you. Choose life!

You'll know the life-giving people because they will foster hope, see potential, and celebrate you as you are. They will work diligently to not separate truth and love. They will not project their fears onto you. They will not project their pain onto you. And they will not project their dreams onto you. And life-giving people are interested in mutual, respectful, joyful friendships.

Beware of people who have no joy...they will resent yours.

Who do you listen to? Whose opinions do you hear... and take in? Are they encouraging, engaging, and elevating to the spirit? Choose well, listen well, and then follow your inspiration...you'll change the world!

Question for reflection: Do you listen more to life-giving or life-taking people?

The Season of Yes!

"What makes the desert beautiful is that it hides, somewhere, a well."

-Antoine de Saint Exupéry

Quick...what's the first word that comes to your mind when you hear "Lent"?

I bet it wasn't "Yes".

The 40 days that precede Easter have typically been known as the Season of "No"; "no chocolate", "no meat", "no coffee", "no television", "no Facebook" (yes, I actually know several people who have given up Facebook for Lent). And saying "no" to things that distract one from responsibilities, that numb one to feelings, that sap life is certainly part of this season. Saying "no" can help us detach from bad habits.

But if all we're doing is saying "no", we're only half way home. Because the "no" won't lead to joy, peace, and growth that lasts.

"No", by itself, stops being sufficient by about age three!

We are meaning-seeking people. We need to have a purpose in mind for why we do what we do, whatever it is. "What is the point of giving up coffee, dessert, meat, or the internet?" "Why am I doing this?" "Am I just following rules to follow rules?" God help us. This is where the "yes" comes in.

Happiness, true happiness, is not just about being free FROM something, it is also about being free FOR something...something more beautiful, more healthy, more loving. "YES."

So the next time you find yourself saying "no", find the "yes" that is attached...and celebrate the good which you are moving toward!

Question for reflection: To affirm the goodness of life, what can you say "Yes" to today?

Bulls-eye!

"Being popular is a dangerous thing."
       -Anonymous

Honestly, I've always found it curious and more than a little disturbing that Christians celebrate so hardily Jesus' "triumphal" entry into Jerusalem. As if we didn't know how hollow, how fleeting, how painfully ironic this reception was.

We wave our palm fronds in the air as the service begins, and then continue fiddling with them as the Gospel message is read. Like we don't know what's coming. Or maybe it's that we do know what's coming, and it's too uncomfortable to sit with.

Five days after being hailed as a King, the Rebel with a Cause would be betrayed and abandoned by his own, scorned, beaten, and prosecuted by the religious and political leaders of his region, and finally nailed to a cross for His efforts. The royal treatment indeed!

Popularity is a dangerous thing. It's dangerous because it sets you up for envy. And hell hath no fury like people who are envious; people who hate you because of who you are and who they are. Popularity places a big bulls-eye right in the middle of your back. But this is not what you should spend time worrying about.

Because the greatest damage is not caused by others, but by oneself.

Forget for a moment being hated for no good reason. What about being "loved" for no good reason?

In my practice I have worked with addictions of every kind, and I promise you nothing has the addictive, seductive power of popularity. How much of a hook is popularity for you? What have you compromised in order to be accepted and liked? What are you still willing to compromise? If pushed, everyone would deep down like to be popular. But at what cost?

In the end, we cannot control what people feel or think about us. However, we can control our *addiction* to what people feel or think about us, remaining focused on who we are and what we are called to do. And this starts by knowing what really matters, and what really doesn't.

Don't spend too much time looking at the crowd. They may love you today, and want to crucify you tomorrow. Keep your eyes on the real prize. That's the lesson of Palm Sunday.

Question for reflection: How much do you compromise in order to be liked?

The Last Time

"Do you love life? Then do not squander time, for that is the stuff life is made of."
    -Benjamin Franklin

In December 1973, the hauntingly beautiful "Time in a Bottle" shot to #1 on the pop charts. Jim Croce had been inspired to write the ballad by and for his infant son. The refrain, *"But there never seems to be enough time to do the things you want to do once you find them,"* expresses a longing that is at once personal and universal. We can all relate, deeply.

And adding to the poignancy of the message was the fact that just three months prior to the song reaching #1, Croce died in an airplane crash. He was thirty, and his son was two.

Time is precious. But it can't be bottled, captured, controlled, and stored up. And it cannot be reclaimed. It is always slipping away, and with it the opportunities we have left to do something meaningful with it. And there never seems to be enough time...

"Do you love life? Then do not squander time, for that is the stuff life is made of."

I think we squander time because we think we can get away with it...that there will always be more. Sort

65

of like a twelve year-old who's just learned how to use dad's ATM card.

How different would our lives be, though, if we approached every situation with the simple question, "What if this is the last time?"

What if this is the last time I kiss my beloved?
What if this is the last time I kneel in prayer?
What if this is the last time I shoot baskets with my son, or belt out a Springsteen song, or dance with my little girl?
What if this is the last time I watch a sunset?

Talk about carpe diem…of suddenly, powerfully living in the moment!

At the end of life, the passage of time is not what's regretted…it's what we've not done with the time we were given that will haunt us.

"What if this is the last time?" Someday it will be… and that'll be o.k. if you've lived well.

Question for reflection: How often do you live IN the moment?

Where Are You Going?

"The future is called 'perhaps,' which is the only
possible thing to call the future."
-Tennessee Williams

"Our faith in the present dies out long before
our faith in the future."
-Ruth Benedict

"We should all be concerned about the future
because we will have to
spend the rest of our lives there."
-Charles F. Kettering

"And in today already walks tomorrow."
-Samuel Taylor Coleridge

Real success

"We make a living by what we get, but we make a life by what we give."
 -Winston Churchill

Benedict Joseph Labre lived in pre-revolution France, struggled with mental illness virtually his entire life, failed each of the eleven times he tried to enter religious life, lost touch with his family, lived as a homeless person for his adult years, subsisted on what he could collect as a beggar, and died of malnutrition at 35 years-old.

Success? Only if you consider sainthood a worthwhile accomplishment.

What is success for you? What does it look like? Honestly. Comfort, professional excellence, the respect of peers, some money, and a solid core of good friends? Yes, a good list. And I wouldn't argue with any of these markers.

Yet St. Benedict Joseph Labre had none of these things. His life reads like a tragic story of failure that makes you want to cry. If he was living today, he'd be the dirty, anonymous, slightly scary-looking man at the bottom of the freeway offramp you try not to make eye contact with as you idle at the red light. Or the shivering corpse in the shadows, bundled up in rags and blankets, you hurry past as you make your way to your car on a cold night.

His life was not exactly the stuff of comic book heroes, or feel-good movies, or popular television.

But that's not ultimately what success is. We can easily lose sight of this in a culture that is so externally oriented, so hell-bent on looking good and feeling superior.

"We make a living by what we get, but we make a life by what we give."

Benedict shared with everyone he met on the pilgrimage routes of Europe; a kind word to the weary, a message of hope to the forlorn, even the food and clothes he'd been given to those who seemed hungrier and colder than he. And when he was attacked and beaten, which happened often, he gave forgiveness.

Success is not about what we collect, what we can count, and what we control. Success is about what we give. It is about the virtue of generosity. And that's what makes Benedict significant. Why he's remembered and revered more than those of his time who had so much. This man gave everything he could, materially and spiritually.

Generosity comes from the Latin root that means "to give birth." And people who practice generosity...

giving their time, their talent, and their treasure… "give birth."

And what is born of generosity? Your legacy…your gift to future generations; that which will live on after you; what you will be remembered best for; what will frame your eternity. If you want to be relevant, if you want your life to matter, give.

Because it's only generosity that will move you from merely "successful" to truly significant.

Question for reflection: How are you generous, and how are you not?

Mothering Day

"The mother's heart is the child's school-room."
-Henry Ward Beecher

Mother's Day is a holy day indeed, a blessed day, a precious day. It is a day we should all celebrate if for no other reason...and there is not a more fundamental reason...than that our mothers chose life. We can and should be forever grateful for this. There is no greater gift.

But on Mother's Day I believe we should also celebrate ALL women who mother, for motherhood is certainly more than a physical act. We miss the true essence of motherhood if we reduce this sacred role to something wholly explained by obstetrics.

Those who mother bear hope.

Those who mother invest in the future.

Those who mother protect innocence.

Those who mother guide the vulnerable.

Those who mother teach about all that really matters.

Those who mother sacrifice for the Good.

Those who mother love and let go...and still love.

Happy Mother's Day, Happy Mothering Day, to all women who carry life, birth life, and nurture life in every way. "Thank you" is a good starting point, but not nearly enough!

Question for reflection: Who has mothered you?

To what end?

"Every man dies. Not every man really lives."
        -William Wallace

St. Maximillian Kolbe, a Franciscan priest, is best known for his heroic death in a starvation bunker in Auschwitz. For many, this is why he's a martyr. But it should really be for how he lived.

Because he was a Catholic priest confronting evil, the Nazis arrested him and sent him to the concentration camp. In July 1941, a man from Kolbe's barracks vanished, prompting the deputy camp commander to pick 10 men from the same barracks to be starved to death in order to deter further escape attempts. One of the selected men, Franciszek Gajowniczek, cried out, "My wife, my children!" It was then that Kolbe volunteered to take his place. No greater love....

After three weeks, all the men in the starvation bunker had died except for Father Kolbe. Finally losing patience with the process, the guards gave him a lethal shot of carbolic acid to finish the job....as if death could silence such a life. Roughly 40 years later, at the canonization ceremony for St. Maximillian, Gajowniczek (the man Kolbe had volunteered to die for) was present and spoke.

Maximillian Kolbe is an obvious example of what we would call a martyr. But as I sat in church this morning, I began reflecting on what he'd say if he was preaching the homily.

And my serious hunch is that he'd focus on what the word martyr means..."witness."

What does your life witness to? Let me put it a different way. Someday, at your funeral, when the nice speeches are finished, and the microphone is turned off, and the niceties around the punch bowl cease. What will people say about your life? What will stand out? What will be remembered?

More than what you died for, martyrdom is about what you lived for.

Question for reflection: What are you living for?

Afflicting and comforting...

"Comfort the afflicted and afflict the comfortable."
  -Finley Peter Dunne

I think we can all readily agree that there are people who need to be afflicted, and those who need to be comforted. The two categories are distinct, no boundary blurring, good and bad? Haves and have-nots? Right?

It seems so easy to identify all the folks who deserve afflicting, who are too comfortable in their sloth. If you're anything like me, your list will be fairly long. Hypocrites, narcissists, materialists, nihilists, self-centered....wow, the labels are flowing wonderfully! Just the thought of getting after them is fun, eh? Deserved. In the name of justice...

It's only slightly bothersome that my affliction list happens to consist entirely of types I don't like.

And what about the afflicted? An easy list to form as well? The homeless, the poor, the under-served; those who are on the fringe, and in danger of falling through the cracks of society.

But what if the "sinners" also need comforting and compassion? And what if the downtrodden need some challenging and some tough love? Now things get interesting...and a lot harder. Because justice moves us

75

toward consistency, and away from biases. Even biases that appear justifiable.

The truth is that the human condition calls for both afflicting and comforting *for all*; the externals can often disguise this truth. However, the greatest poverty is not material but spiritual. One can be selfish with or without possessions. And the most profound brokenness is interior.

We need to be clear about what justice is before we start trying to dish it out. Justice is about fairness, no double standards, afflicting and comforting in truth *and* love ... everyone.

And we'd do well to start with our selves!

Question for reflection: Where are the double standards in my life?

Lessons from Libya

"There never was a war that was not inward."
    -Marianne Moore

Freedom cannot be separated from responsibility. This is an eternal truth that transcends culture, race, geopolitics, and religion.

I understood this once again as I watched the latest crisis unfolding in Libya; from the protesters risking their lives in the streets of Tripoli, to the Libyan pilots refusing to follow orders to bomb their own people, to the Libyan Ambassador to the United Nations denouncing the madman who has held Libya captive for far too long.

But today's Libya was last week's Egypt, and last month's Iraq, and last year's Afghanistan, and so on, and so on. There has always been war, and until the end of time there will be.

What shouldn't be missed is the intimate relationship between freedom and responsibility, an existential challenge to every human heart, but never revealed more clearly than in times of great crisis.

To be fully human, to choose life, we must first recognize that we are free. And that in our freedom we are called to respond well...to respond in ways that support the dignity and worth of self and others. This is most human.

The protesters, the pilots, and the ambassador are heroic examples, no doubt. I am inspired by them, I celebrate them, and I pray for them. But the greatest revolutions, the most profound battles, are not captured on television.

The virtuous life, the life grounded in freedom and responsibility, is won or lost in a thousand little "wars" every day. In the home and at work, in the classroom and on the playground, in emails and in texts; we are free to choose truth or lies, kindness or callousness, generosity or selfishness...peace or violence. And our consciences tell us that we must answer, sooner or later, for the choices we make.

God help those who struggle tonight in the Middle East, and God help the rest of us as well.

Question for reflection: What "inner war" do you need to focus on in your life, in order to become more free and responsible?

Men being men

"The crisis of the Modern age is the crisis of fatherhood."
   -Benedict XVI

All men are called to be fathers. For some, this will include a biological process, but the virtue of fatherhood is so much more than that. All men are called to be fathers. Oh, would this world be a better place if that truth was understood.

Being a father is not simply a state one finds one's self in...at least it shouldn't be for long. Fatherhood is a way of being in the world; a personal and existential commitment to the future. It is about being generous with one's time and experience, and teaching with words, but also by example. Fatherhood asks one to sacrifice for the good, to protect innocence, to respond proactively to the emotional and spiritual needs of others, and to care deeply about life.

Fatherhood is essential to becoming a real man.

Today I had the opportunity to speak on the topic of Fatherhood at a men's conference. The participants were there not because it was court-ordered, or work-ordered. There was no immediate gratification or external benefit, and on a cold, rainy Saturday it wasn't even convenient.

These men were there because they wanted to be better men, plain and simple. They wanted to be better equipped to love, and guide, and encourage others... and they understood deeply that the young are our hope, and that every child matters.

I think these men are heroes.

Question for reflection: How do you define a "real man"?

Even flies

"All the efforts of the human mind cannot exhaust the essence of a single fly."
      -St. Thomas Aquinas

Labels can be very helpful when shopping for a car, or a computer, or a pair of shoes. They help us organize information and make efficient and generally informed decisions. I know if I buy a Volvo, I'll get a safe car; a Mac, and I'll have a trustworthy computer; Cole-Haan, a quality pair of loafers.

But how meaningful are labels when applied to human beings: white, black, believers, non-believers, liberals, conservatives, rich, poor? Is this enough information to really know the individual person you're trying to cubby-hole? White people are racists. Christians are anti-intellectual. Liberals are atheists. Poor people are lazy. To the reasonable person, these too-broad generalizations, stereotypes, are quickly seen as both ridiculous and unkind.

Yet, we've all felt pre-judged, categorized, and rejected based on superficial information that reduces us to demographic categories. And few things hurt more. This doesn't stop us, however, from being tempted to do the same thing to others. There really is some truth to the adage that we abuse the way we've been abused.

Labeling people serves a kind of protective function, which is why it's done so regularly. We want to know who's safe and who's not, who's reliable and who's not, who's good, and who's not. And we want to know quickly, and we really don't want there to be any gray area, any room for process and discovery, any mystery. Too much risk and up-front investment.

This is fundamentally fear-based and un-natural. Understandable, but unnatural…because it is not grounded in Love.

"All the efforts of the human mind cannot exhaust the essence of a single fly." This from St. Thomas Aquinas, arguably the greatest genius of the last millennium. If anyone understood the powers and limits of the human mind, it was the Angelic Doctor. So, if we can't figure out the essence of a fly, what do you think the chances are that we'll be able to fully plumb the mystery of a human being made in the Image of God?

Should we, then, stop trying to think, stop trying to reason, stop trying to figure things out? Of course not. Heaven knows this world could use a little more rationality, and a little less hysteria.

But it does mean that as we live our lives, and try (more days than not) to get along with those around us, we'd do well to respect the dimension of mystery in others, and to practice reason with a good measure of humility and awe!

Question for reflection: How often do you avoid loving by labeling?

82

The Need for Heroes

"As you get older it is harder to have heroes, but it is sort of necessary."
        -Ernest Hemingway

Yes, it is harder to have heroes as we grow older. We hear, read, and see things we are (thankfully) sheltered from in childhood. And we are hurt. And then we get a little bit harder.

Of course no one is perfect. No one comes through every time, for everyone, in all situations (for the purpose of this discussion, Jesus does not count). But this is how we define "hero" when we are children...sort of a mix between Superman and God.

We discover one day that heroes are human. And in this inevitable loss of innocence, we tend to turn toward doubt. And here lies the problem. In our anger, our disappointment, our disillusionment, we accept the notion that one cannot have heroes. It's protective, usually, and not even a fully conscious choice...but we don't want to feel let down again, betrayed. And many of us never turn back.

Yet we must have heroes, and not just as children. It is, as Hemingway wrote, necessary. Necessary? Like water and oxygen are necessary to sustain life? No. But necessary in order to sustain emotional and spiritual growth.

We will always need examples, inspirations, models, for how to live. We need to see the Good (even if it is not presented in its wholeness) if we are to combat the crushing, dehumanizing, killing effect of doubt.

If we are to develop as human beings, we cannot let doubt reign in our hearts. It feeds selfishness, and fear, and cynicism. It's the psychological equivalent of a black hole.

Most heroes will have a particular gift or two that they live out with great brilliance; the virtue of courage, or generosity, or creativity, or perseverance. And their light will inspire others to be more, and do more. And the world becomes a little brighter. These men and women will not be perfect, but that's not what heroes are.

I believe that we can be well-grounded in reality and still celebrate the ideal when we see it. Hero-worship must pass with the naivete of childhood, but emulation of those who live out particular virtues in heroic ways cannot, must not.

The world needs more hope, and less despair, more faith and less fear. Find what you admire, what you want to become, what is truly beautiful and good. And then see that these qualities reside in a human being.

Celebrate the heroic, re-consider having a hero or two, and maybe in this process become one yourself!

Question for reflection: Who would you consider heroes?

What IS your duty?

"Let's have faith that right makes might; and in that faith let us, to the end, dare to do our duty as we understand it."
     -Abraham Lincoln

Do you believe this is true? That right makes might? That living a life dedicated to doing the right thing can actually make a difference in this tired, weary world? If you do, then knowing WHAT your duty is becomes that much more crucial.

Duty. What does that word mean anymore? It is not commonly used nowadays, save for commercials about the military. And most assuredly the brave men and women who serve in our military do their duty in particular and sacrificial ways. But of course the great Mr. Lincoln's challenge to "dare to do our duty" extends beyond military service.

What do you understand to be YOUR duty? As a husband or wife, as a mother or father, as a friend or co-worker, as a neighbor? How do you begin to understand this key to TRUE power?

I believe your duty, my duty, humankind's duty, is to "dare to do good." This is the foundation everything else we do should build on.

Start with the acknowledgement that you can make a difference. YOU CAN MAKE A DIFFERENCE. If you truly, deeply, passionately believe this, then the daring will naturally follow...the daring to take the extra step, to care just a bit more, and to put love into action in a thousand little ways. You don't need to find a cure for cancer, or win the Nobel peace prize, or be the greatest president in our nation's history. You simply need to believe that right makes might...and then do the right thing, more often than not.

You know what the good is, what the right thing is. It's what you learned in kindergarten, and what your heart tells you is true when you are still. Be kind, be honest, share what you have, and play well with others.

And remember that truly good people don't get that way by doing one thing 100% better. They become truly good by doing one hundred things 1% better. Because goodness is contagious.

Right makes might; live like this is true, and watch it become so.

Question for reflection: What do you consider your duty to be?

Understanding Happiness

"Happiness is secured through virtue; it is a good attained by man's own will."
          -Thomas Aquinas

"I just want to be happy." "I just want my partner to be happy." "I just want my kids to be happy."

In therapy and outside of therapy, happiness is the goal I hear more people talk about than any other. And there's nothing wrong with this goal. In fact, I think it's an excellent goal to strive for!

The problem isn't the goal, the problem is in how people try and achieve the goal.

We live in a world that consistently misunderstands what makes one happy. We will be happy, or so our reality T.V. culture tells us, when we have more money, or popularity, or plastic surgery, or power, or alcohol, or sex, or experiences.

Being able to better control things and people around us would help a lot too, right?

"Winning", I guess.

The lie is that happiness can somehow be found apart from good behavior; that it can be bought, or manufactured, or manipulated with enough "fun."

Fun will sustain happiness about as well as cotton candy sustains a starving person. Fun is great, but it is not the source of happiness.

St. Thomas reminds us that happiness cannot be separated from virtue...good habits. And happiness is the product of good living, plain and simple; no short cuts.

We will never be happier then when we are using our freedom to do good and be good. It sounds too easy, and perhaps too boring, to lead to happiness.

And if you judge happiness by one night, or one weekend, or one month, the connection between goodness and happiness may not be clear.

But study the people you know who are truly, deeply, securely happy, and you will find lives marked by generosity, kindness, peace, balance, love, and courage; virtue.

Happiness, in the end, is not a great mystery. Do good, surround yourself with good people, and don't give in to cynicism.

You'll change your world, and you'll change THE world. And yes, you'll have a lot of fun, too.

Question for reflection: Are you a happy person?

One man's trash...

"Ring the bells that still can ring,
Forget your perfect offering.
There is a crack in everything.
That's how the light gets in."
    -Leonard Cohen

Antique stores are hopeful places, places that believe in second chances. They accept what others have thrown away, given up on, discarded as un-useable, because they see the potential that remains. Recently, I found myself in a dusty and well-stocked one named *"One Man's Trash..."*, an homage to the saying, "One man's trash is another man's treasure."

This store had a little of everything, from automobile parts, to farming and gardening equipment, to knick-knacks and artwork found in households. I struck up a conversation with the older gentleman who owned the store, wondering what he enjoyed most about the antiques business. "I believe that everything can be used again, and nothing needs to be wasted," he said with a contented smile. "I love that notion."

[handwritten margin note: This is a junk store - not an antique store!]

Everything is useful, and nothing needs to be wasted.

But shame tells us something different. Shame tells us that there's something so fundamentally wrong with us, so unforgiveable and ugly that if anyone really knew

89

us fully, they'd be repulsed. And we've accepted this version of the story to one degree or another. So we feel we must hide those parts of ourselves, and pray no one ever finds out.

Maybe the shame is connected to things you've done; choices you regret so deeply that you've mistaken who you are for what you did. And no good can come from this.

Maybe the shame is about something that was done to you; and the trauma has left you feeling like you're too broken to ever be whole again. And no good can come from this.

Unchecked and unexamined, shame feeds on isolation and secrets. Its power grows in the dark.

But did you ever stop to think that only humans feel shame? Animals don't feel shame. Fish and plants don't feel shame. Bugs don't feel shame.

Because only humans can sin.

What if we could do something different with shame; to understand it's presence *as a confirmation of our inherent worth and our potential for transformation?* Stay with me here.

Shame confirms two truths: that we are not living as we should, and that we are meant for more. Yes, we're wounded, but we can heal. Yes, we're imperfect, but we can learn. Yes we're human, but we're *human…* made in the Image of God.

The truth is that if we really were worthless, and so horribly flawed that we could not heal or be loved, *we wouldn't feel shame.* We'd feel right at home in our garbage. Our negative self-concept would be congruent with who we truly were, and who we were capable of being. But we don't…and shame tells us we shouldn't.

Feelings of shame tell us that we're stuck in a reality that isn't fit for us. We are built for freedom, for dignity, for joy, and anything less is not going to feel natural. *Everything* is useful, and nothing should be wasted.

It's the ultimate recycling plan.

Question for reflection: What have you felt ashamed of in your life, and what have you done about it?

Don't give up

I want to start with one of my favorite statements of faith.

"Anyway"
People are often unreasonable, illogical and self-centered;
Forgive them anyway.
If you are kind, people may accuse you of selfish, ulterior
motives;
Be kind anyway.
If you are successful, you will win some false friends and some
true enemies;
Succeed anyway.
If you are honest and frank, people may cheat you;
Be honest and frank anyway.
What you spend years building, someone could destroy
overnight;
Build anyway.
If you find serenity and happiness, they may be jealous;
Be happy anyway.
The good you do today, people will often forget tomorrow;
Do good anyway.
Give the world the best you have, and it may never be enough;
Give the world the best you've got anyway.
You see, in the final analysis, it is between you and your God;
It was never between you and them anyway.
-Bd. Mother Teresa of Calcutta

Detachment is a virtue that in the 21st century is mis-
understood and seriously undervalued. The word itself

is problematic, sounding too much like "detached".... checked-out, bored, impersonal, distant. But the virtue of detachment is anything but.

Detachment helps us get at the "why" question. Why do good? Why persevere? Why hope? Why love? And detachment purifies intentions as well, helping us see our own unfinished business: pride, dependency on the approval of others, control, and unrealistic expectations about how life and people SHOULD be.

Easier said than done! From an early age we are taught about the importance of justice, of fairness. And in a JUST world, things would be fair. People would be nice to you when you were nice to them. People would be generous with you when you were generous with them. People would be truthful with you when you were truthful with them. But of course life isn't fair. People are not always nice, generous, truthful. We know this, and yet the fantasy is so hard to give up. If I just try harder, people will do the right thing. Sometimes. Just enough to keep you hooked into the false belief that your effort at goodness is enough to make everything fair.

It's not. And that's o.k. In fact it's better than o.k., it's necessary. Because as Mother Teresa reminds us IT ISN'T ABOUT YOU AND THEM in the end. It's about you and your Creator. It's about you becoming the person you were meant to be. It's about you growing up.

Let go, detach....NOT from people, but from illusions about people, NOT from this world, but from illusions about this world, and NOT from the struggle to be good, but from illusions about the magical power of goodness.

Your daily efforts to make the world a better place, however big or small, matter more than you know. Humans being human doesn't change this truth one iota. Detach from all that needs to be given up, but don't give up.

Question for reflection: What do you need to let go of, in order to keep moving forward?

Making beautiful music

"It is good to have an end to journey toward; but it is the journey that matters in the end."
        -Ursula K. LeGuin

If you've ever gone to hear an orchestra play, you know that the performance doesn't begin until the musicians first tune their instruments. The oboe sounds the note "A", and players make sure their instruments match the pitch. It's the "warm-up" if you will. Many balmy summer evenings I've sat in the amphitheater at the Hollywood Bowl as the sun sank below the hills, and listened to the orchestra slowly but surely get in tune. This delights me in ways I can't fully explain.

Thus, I could thoroughly relate when a friend told me about his son's response to the same experience. The young man was attending the Bowl for the first time, and his parents got him there in time to soak in the atmosphere of the place, and watch the orchestra tuning up; kind of preparation for the "real show." After the concert, on the way home, they excitedly asked the boy which part of the performance he liked best. "Oh," he replied, "The beginning, just before the guy with the stick came out."

The process of orchestral tuning *is* fascinating! The musicians come on stage as individuals, playing various melodies and rhythms. There are moments of discordant sound, and of back and forth between the sections when it's hard to imagine anything like beautiful music is possible. It's more a cacophony of noise than a symphony of sound!

Then the "guy with the stick" (aka the conductor!) enters, and with a wave of the arm the many blend into one cohesive unit. The different sections, the string and woodwind, brass and percussion complement each other, and communicate the full message that is too deep for words.

And that lasts 24 hours.

The very next evening the orchestra will begin the process all over again. These world-class musicians will each come back on stage as individual parts, play, stop and listen, play some more, and make adjustments until they finally find unity. Orchestral tuning is a good metaphor for life.

There will be times when your world is in perfect pitch; everything has come together, you feel wonderful, you think lofty thoughts, and beautiful music is made. Then there will be periods when you feel splintered, your emotions are at war, and you think that snapping your conductor's baton in two and storming off the stage might be the best plan of all.

But most of the time you'll be somewhere in-between; happiness and sadness, joy and sorrow, peace and anger.

There will be this strange mix of thoughts and feelings that you get to somehow make sense of. This is pretty normal. Growth and healing is a 24-hour miracle… one day at a time. Don't be surprised by the process; and maybe even get to the point where you accept it.

Because in real life the concert *is* the tuning and the adjusting.

Question for reflection: What are your expectations about life?

Made in the USA
Charleston, SC
05 November 2011